A TRUE BOOK™

NATURAL DISASTER!

All About Tornadoes

Discovering Earth's Strongest Winds

Cody Crane

Children's Press®
An imprint of Scholastic Inc.

Content Consultant
Dr. Kristen Rasmussen
Assistant Professor
Department of Atmospheric Science
Colorado State University

Library of Congress Cataloging-in-Publication Data
Names: Crane, Cody, author.
Title: All about tornadoes / by Cody Crane.
Description: First edition. | New York : Children's Press, an imprint of Scholastic Inc., 2021. | Series: A true
   book: natural disaster! | Includes bibliographical references and index. | Audience: Ages 8–10. | Audience:
   Grades 4–6. | Summary: "This book shows readers the awesome power of tornadoes"— Provided by publisher.
Identifiers: LCCN 2021003960 (print) | LCCN 2021003961 (ebook) | ISBN 9781338769616 (library binding) |
   ISBN 9781338769623 (paperback) | ISBN 9781338769630 (ebook)
Subjects: LCSH: Tornadoes—Juvenile literature. | Natural disasters—Juvenile literature.
Classification: LCC QC955.2 .C73 2021 (print) | LCC QC955.2 (ebook) | DDC 551.55/3—dc23
LC record available at https://lccn.loc.gov/2021003960
LC ebook record available at https://lccn.loc.gov/2021003961

10 9 8 7 6 5 4 3 2 1   22 23 24 25 26

Printed in the U.S.A. 113
First edition, 2022

Series produced by Priyanka Lamichhane
Book design by Kathleen Petelinsek
Illustrations on pages 42–43 by Gary LaCoste

**Front cover: Background: A large tornado spins across a field;
top: A house is destroyed by a tornado; top right: The formation
of a large supercell thunderstorm; bottom: A car is crushed by a
tree in the aftermath of a tornado.**

**Back cover: Dark storm clouds cover the sky as a
tornado touches down over a green field.**

A TRUE BOOK™

NATURAL DISASTER!

All About Tornadoes

Discovering Earth's Strongest Winds

Cody Crane

SCHOLASTIC

Find the Truth!

Everything you are about to read is true *except* for one of the sentences on this page.

Which one is **TRUE**?

T or F   More tornadoes are reported in the United States than in any other country.

T or F   Tornadoes are most likely to appear at dawn.

Find the answers in this book.

What's in This Book?

A home is
destroyed after
being struck by
a tornado.

A tornado spins behind some trees as it approaches a road in Nebraska.

The **BIG** Truth

Chasing Tornadoes

4 Tragedy Strikes

5 Staying Safe

A water spout, or tornado over water, forms on the island of Malapascua in the Philippines.

Blown Away

The date was March 18, 1925. The forecast called for some rain and wind across the midwestern United States. So, people were surprised when, in the early afternoon, storm clouds began to appear. What came next was even more unexpected. Around 1 p.m., a spinning funnel-shaped cloud about one mile (1.6 kilometers) wide dropped from the sky. It was a tornado.

The tornado touched down near the town of Ellington, Missouri, and headed northeast. Its 300-mile-per-hour (483-kilometer-per-hour) destructive winds demolished the towns of Annapolis and Biehle in Missouri.

It then crossed the Mississippi River into Illinois, and then into Indiana. It destroyed several towns across both states.

After traveling for three and a half hours across 219 miles (352 km), the tornado finally died out. Along with causing lots of property damage, the tornado killed 695 people and injured 2,000. The tornado, which became known as the Tri-State Tornado, was the longest-lasting and farthest-traveling tornado ever recorded in the United States.

Many buildings were damaged or destroyed by the Tri-State Tornado of 1925.

As a tornado approaches, it makes a roaring noise, similar to a train speeding through a tunnel.

The "twist" of this tornado can be seen as it bends to one side while spinning through a field.

Terrible Twisters

Tornadoes, also called twisters, have the strongest winds on Earth. Their winds can reach 300 miles per hour (483 kph). Tornadoes form when a spinning column of air called a **vortex** reaches from storm clouds in the sky down to the ground. Tornadoes move as they spin, sweeping up anything in their paths. They can toss cars and trees through the air, and even level entire towns.

The Making of a Tornado

Tornadoes often occur in the area between two colliding air masses. This region is known as a **front**. One of the air masses contains cool, dry air; the other contains warm, moist air. When the air masses meet, they can mix to form large, violent thunderstorms called **supercells**. Air does not rotate inside most thunderstorms, but it does inside a supercell. This is why they are the most likely storms to spawn tornadoes.

A supercell is usually round, with a flat bottom and a trailing edge that juts out.

Supercells are not the only storms that can spawn tornadoes. Hurricanes can spawn them, too.

Inside a Supercell

About 20 percent of supercells form tornadoes.
Take a look at what happens inside one of these storms.

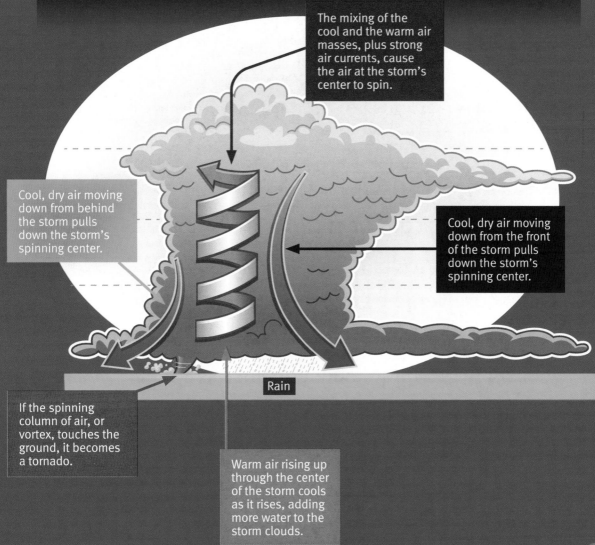

The mixing of the cool and the warm air masses, plus strong air currents, cause the air at the storm's center to spin.

Cool, dry air moving down from behind the storm pulls down the storm's spinning center.

Cool, dry air moving down from the front of the storm pulls down the storm's spinning center.

If the spinning column of air, or vortex, touches the ground, it becomes a tornado.

Rain

Warm air rising up through the center of the storm cools as it rises, adding more water to the storm clouds.

In 2013, winds from a tornado in El Reno, Oklahoma, wrapped this car around a tree.

Packing a Punch

Tornadoes last an average of three minutes. They do not travel far, either. The average distance covered by most tornadoes is about 3.5 miles (5.6 km). And they are not always large. An average tornado measures just 328 feet (100 meters) across, about the length of a football field. But a tornado's size does not always relate to its strength. Even the smallest can cause a huge amount of damage.

Twisters Over Water

Sometimes, a tornado forms or moves over a body of water, such as an ocean or a lake. This type of tornado is called a waterspout. Waterspouts do not suck up or spew out water. They are spinning columns of air, like normal tornadoes. Waterspouts are usually weaker than typical tornadoes, but they can still pose a risk to boats and ships. And they can move onto land, posing a risk to people onshore.

Waterspouts have been known to lift seaweed and animals such as fish into the sky.

Some waterspouts develop from the water's surface upward. Tornadoes form from the sky downward.

The Asian country of Bangladesh has more tornado deaths per year than any other country.

The 1989 Daulatpur–Saturia tornado in Bangladesh is the deadliest on record.

Touchdown Hot Spots

Tornadoes have been reported on every continent except Antarctica. But by far, the most reports are in the United States. According to those reports, the United States experiences about 1,000 tornadoes per year. Canada reports the second-greatest number, about 100 per year.

Tornado Alley

Most tornadoes in the United States form in a region known as "Tornado Alley." It includes several states in the Great Plains. This flat area of land stretches across the center of the country. Tornado Alley is located in a spot where cold air moving south from Canada meets warm, moist air moving north from the Gulf of Mexico, and sometimes dry air from the Rocky Mountains. This creates a front and provides the perfect weather conditions for tornadoes to form.

The Great Plains, seen here during a thunderstorm, stretches as far as the eye can see.

More Than One Alley?

Tornado Alley is not the only tornado-prone area in the United States. There are actually multiple alleys in different parts of the country where unstable storm systems often create tornadoes. These include Dixie Alley in the South, Carolina Alley in the Southeast, and Hoosier Alley in the Midwest.

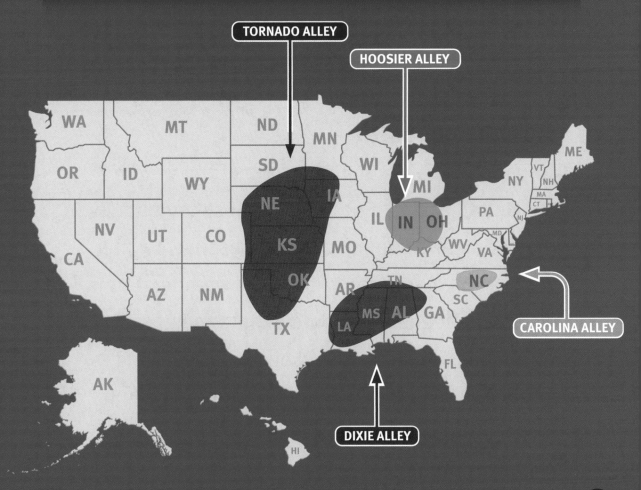

A large tornado spins through trees and approaches a wet road near York, Nebraska. It was spotted in the early evening, around 6 p.m.

Tornado Season

Tornadoes can occur at any time of the year in the United States. But they are most common in the spring and summer. This is because warmer weather increases the chances of thunderstorms, which are needed to produce tornadoes. Tornadoes are also most likely to appear from 3 to 9 p.m. Why? By the late afternoon, the sun has heated the **atmosphere** enough for storm clouds to form.

Tornado Outbreak!

Some storms are so large that they can create dozens or even hundreds of tornadoes. A tornado outbreak is when six or more tornadoes spawn from the same storm. Outbreaks can span large areas. For example, the 2020 Easter outbreak in the United States spawned twisters across 10 different states, from Texas to Maryland. Tornadoes that form during an outbreak usually all happen on the same day.

Two tornadoes spin toward the town of Pilger, Nebraska, in June 2014. Two tornadoes that touch down at the same time are also called "twin tornadoes."

Most tornadoes in the
United States move in a
similar direction—northeast—
once they touch down.

Scientists use mobile
weather labs to study
tornadoes in the field.

Tornado Trackers

Scientists who study weather are called **meteorologists**. They monitor Earth's atmosphere. This includes keeping an eye on developing storms that could produce tornadoes. Predicting exactly when and where tornadoes will touch down is difficult. Meteorologists rely on high-tech tools to detect tornadoes. They also use models of the atmosphere to predict tornado formation to alert anyone who is in the possible path of a twister.

Watching the Weather

A meteorologist's main tool for tracking tornadoes is **Doppler radar**. It sends energy waves into the atmosphere. The waves bounce off objects, such as raindrops, to detect storms. Doppler radar can also measure the speed and motion of **precipitation** within a storm. This can reveal the direction a storm is moving and the strength of its winds. If Doppler radar senses rotating winds in a storm, it could mean a tornado is forming.

The National Weather Service operates about 150 Doppler radars across the United States.

How to Measure a Tornado

The Enhanced Fujita Scale estimates a tornado's wind speed based on how destructive it is. It assigns a tornado a rating from EF0 to EF5, with EF0 being the weakest and EF5 being the strongest. The "EF" stands for "Enhanced Fujita."

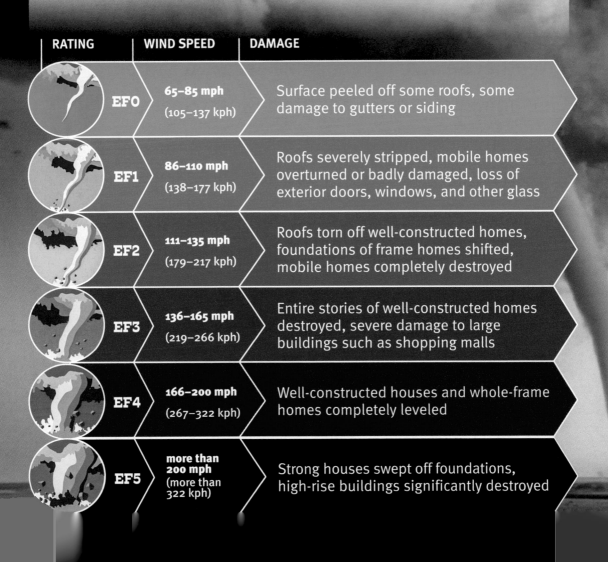

RATING	WIND SPEED	DAMAGE
EF0	65–85 mph (105–137 kph)	Surface peeled off some roofs, some damage to gutters or siding
EF1	86–110 mph (138–177 kph)	Roofs severely stripped, mobile homes overturned or badly damaged, loss of exterior doors, windows, and other glass
EF2	111–135 mph (179–217 kph)	Roofs torn off well-constructed homes, foundations of frame homes shifted, mobile homes completely destroyed
EF3	136–165 mph (219–266 kph)	Entire stories of well-constructed homes destroyed, severe damage to large buildings such as shopping malls
EF4	166–200 mph (267–322 kph)	Well-constructed houses and whole-frame homes completely leveled
EF5	more than 200 mph (more than 322 kph)	Strong houses swept off foundations, high-rise buildings significantly destroyed

Storm Spotters

Dark storm clouds, hail, and a greenish-colored sky are signs tornadoes could be on the way.

Along with radar data, meteorologists also rely on local "Storm Spotters" to watch for tornadoes. These volunteers are trained by the U.S. National Weather Service to recognize severe weather, including tornado conditions. Storm Spotters keep their communities safe by watching and providing reports to the weather service. The information helps meteorologists give timely and accurate tornado warnings.

Storm Spotter volunteers often include police, firefighters, and emergency workers.

Tools of the Trade

Along with Doppler radar and eyewitness reports, meteorologists use many other tools to study stormy weather that could unleash tornadoes.

Thermometer: A tool that measures air temperature; the temperature drops during a tornado.

Barometer: A tool with a rotating needle (or fluid) that measures air **pressure**.

Anemometer: A spinning device used to measure wind speed.

Computer: This tool is used to analyze data and run models to predict tornadoes.

Notification systems: Tools including social media, email, texts, and apps give warnings.

Chasing Tornadoes

Tornadoes are unpredictable, short-lived, and dangerous. This makes them difficult to study. But that does not stop some brave scientists who get up close to tornadoes in order to collect data. Their goal is to improve tornado forecasts to help save lives. Here are some of the tools they use to do just that.

Weather Vehicles: Scientists follow tornadoes in heavy-duty trucks and SUVs. These are outfitted with weather-tracking equipment, such as video cameras, mobile Doppler radar, and other weather instruments. Radios allow the scientists to talk to each other, while GPS tracks a storm's location.

Balloons: Some scientists release weather balloons that carry instruments to measure air pressure, moisture, wind speed and direction, and temperature. Other researchers place containers filled with weather sensors in the path of tornadoes.

Drones: Meteorologists are now testing brand-new tools. They fly remote-controlled **drones** into supercell thunderstorms to gather data about how tornadoes form.

Tornadoes have hit many major U.S. cities, including Atlanta, Chicago, Dallas, Miami, and New York.

A tornado struck St. Louis, Missouri, in 2011, damaging thousands of homes.

Tragedy Strikes

About 70 percent of tornadoes are weak and cause little damage. They are more likely to form in rural areas where there are few people or buildings. However, powerful twisters do touch down near populated towns or cities once in a while. There, they can cause a huge amount of death and destruction. Here are some recent tornadoes that have had a major impact in the United States.

2011 Super Outbreak

From April 25 to 28, 2011, a storm system swept across more than 12 U.S. states, from Texas to New York. The system's storms caused severe flooding and produced a whopping 362 tornadoes. It was the largest tornado outbreak on record. Alabama and Mississippi were the worst affected. Arkansas, Georgia, Tennessee, and Virginia also suffered damage. In all, the outbreak resulted in the deaths of 321 people and injured nearly 3,000.

Before

After

The 2011 Super Outbreak hit heavily populated areas, such as Tuscaloosa, Alabama. It caused a total of $11 billion in damage.

Then-President Barack Obama visited survivors in Joplin, Missouri, after a tornado struck the town.

2011 Joplin Tornado

On Sunday, May 22, 2011, a powerful EF5 tornado struck the town of Joplin, Missouri. The tornado destroyed a large portion of the town. It was the single deadliest U.S. tornado in more than 60 years, causing the deaths of 162 people. It was also the costliest single tornado on record, causing $2.8 billion in damage. The tornado was part of a larger outbreak that spawned a total of 241 tornadoes and lasted five days.

El Reno Tornado

On Friday, May 31, 2013, the largest tornado ever seen touched down near El Reno, Oklahoma. It stretched 2.6 miles (4.2 km) wide with winds reaching about 300 mph (483 kph). The U.S. National Weather Service called it "the most dangerous tornado in storm-observing history." It missed the populated area of Oklahoma City, but it still destroyed parts of El Reno.

Timeline of Deadly Tornadoes

1551
A waterspout hits the harbor in the European country of Malta, destroying a fleet of warships.

1851
A pair of waterspouts move onto land in Italy and become two intense tornadoes, killing at least 500 people.

1908
A tornado cuts a path through Omaha, Nebraska, destroying or damaging about 2,000 homes.

1936
A powerful tornado hits Tupelo, Mississippi. It sweeps away homes and levels entire neighborhoods.

1551

1908

1936

Weird Weather

Even after tornadoes touch down, it is hard to know how they will behave. Twisters can destroy one house but not those next to it. They can pick up fragile items and carry them great distances, leaving them unharmed. Or they can do the opposite. Tornadoes can sweep away anything in their path. They can turn any object, from trees to cars, into deadly **projectiles**. Flying debris is the most common cause of death from tornadoes.

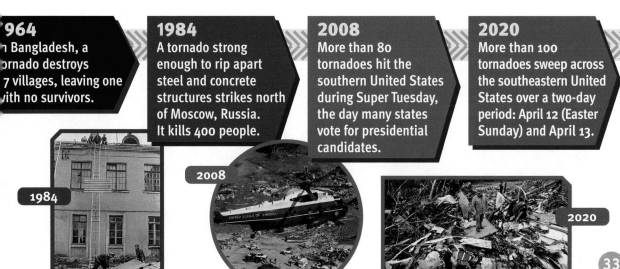

1964
In Bangladesh, a tornado destroys 7 villages, leaving one with no survivors.

1984
A tornado strong enough to rip apart steel and concrete structures strikes north of Moscow, Russia. It kills 400 people.

2008
More than 80 tornadoes hit the southern United States during Super Tuesday, the day many states vote for presidential candidates.

2020
More than 100 tornadoes sweep across the southeastern United States over a two-day period: April 12 (Easter Sunday) and April 13.

1984

2008

2020

During a tornado, people should duck and cover, or kneel down and shield their head with their hands.

In places where tornadoes are common, schools practice drills so students know what to do during a storm.

Staying Safe

In most tornado-prone areas, there are safety measures in place to protect people. Some cities have warning sirens to alert residents of a nearby twister. Officials also send texts to phones and broadcast emergency information on local radio and TV channels. During a tornado, the best thing for people to do is seek shelter. Hospitals, malls, and other large buildings often have protected areas where people can ride out a storm.

A storm cellar is a type of underground structure built to withstand severe weather.

Most storm cellars have a slanted door that allows debris to slide off and blow over it, so the door does not get blocked.

Seeking Shelter

Basements or storm cellars are the safest places to go during a tornado. The next best place is a central room, closet, or hallway on the lowest floor away from windows. It's also important to get under something sturdy. Heavy tables or mattresses can act as shields when there is flying debris. Tornadoes can damage mobile homes. Some are not secured to the ground. People living in them should find safer shelter.

Tornado Alerts

The U.S. National Weather Service sends alerts before tornadoes. There are three types of alerts depending on how likely it is that a tornado will hit. The weakest is a Tornado Watch (1), then a Tornado Warning (2). The strongest is a Tornado Emergency (3).

1

Tornado WATCH

2

Tornado WARNING

3

Tornado EMERGENCY

MEANING

The conditions are right for severe thunderstorms and tornadoes to develop.

A developing tornado has been detected.

A destructive tornado is on the ground and headed toward a populated area.

WHAT YOU SHOULD DO

- Listen for tornado sirens.

- Pay attention to text alerts and local news for more information.

- Keep an eye on weather conditions.

- Locate members of your family. Check emergency supplies and review where to shelter.

- Seek shelter in a pre-planned location.

- Pay attention to text alerts and local news for weather updates.

- Do not leave your shelter area until the warning is lifted.

- Take cover immediately.

- If you are in a car, it cannot outrace a tornado. Park it and take shelter in the nearest building, ditch, or drainage tunnel.

- Stay away from objects that could be sent flying by strong winds.

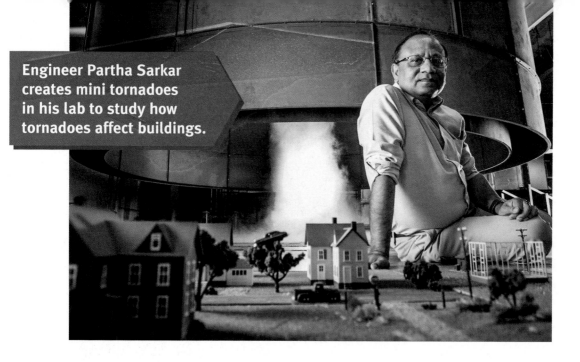

Engineer Partha Sarkar creates mini tornadoes in his lab to study how tornadoes affect buildings.

Disaster-Proof?

At Iowa State University, engineers test ways to build homes that can better withstand high winds to keep people safe during tornadoes. Their lab uses a large metal tube with a powerful fan on top to create small twisters. The scientists see how these fake tornadoes affect a town full of model buildings. They have found that tornadoes often damage roofs. Making roofs stronger could protect buildings and the people inside them.

Better Prepared

Tornadoes continue to be one of the most destructive forces on Earth. But thanks to improved forecasting and earlier warnings, more people than ever are staying safe during these storms. Even though twisters seem to appear out of nowhere and wreak havoc at random, there is a science behind these tornadoes. The more we learn about them, the better we can prepare to face these incredibly powerful winds.

Sending cell phone alerts ahead of an approaching tornado saves lives.

U.S. Tornadoes

Scientists have learned that certain areas of the United States experience greater tornadic activity than others. Study the map showing the average number of tornadoes that hit each state each year, and then answer the questions that follow.

Analyze It!

1 Which state is hit by tornadoes most often?

2 Which states experience fewer than three tornadoes on average?

3 Do more tornadoes occur on the East Coast or the West Coast?

4 What is the average number of tornadoes per year in each of the states that mainly fall in the Tornado Alley? For guidance, go back to the map on page 17.

Average Number of Tornadoes Per Year in the United States

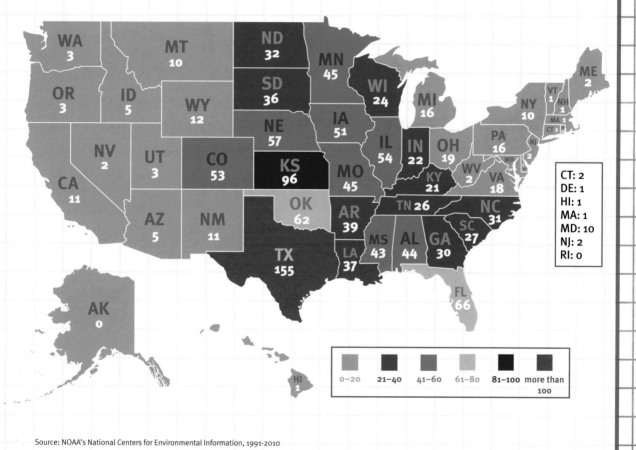

WA	3
MT	10
ND	32
MN	45
ME	2
OR	3
ID	5
WY	12
SD	36
WI	24
MI	16
VT	1
NH	1
NY	10
NV	2
UT	3
CO	53
NE	57
IA	51
IL	54
IN	22
OH	19
PA	16
CA	11
KS	96
MO	45
KY	21
WV	2
VA	18
AZ	5
NM	11
OK	62
AR	39
TN	26
NC	31
MS	43
AL	44
GA	30
SC	27
TX	155
LA	37
AK	0
FL	66
HI	1

CT: 2
DE: 1
HI: 1
MA: 1
MD: 10
NJ: 2
RI: 0

Legend: 0–20 | 21–40 | 41–60 | 61–80 | 81–100 | more than 100

Source: NOAA's National Centers for Environmental Information, 1991-2010

ANSWERS: 1. Texas 2. Alaska, Connecticut, Delaware, Hawaii, Massachusetts, Maine, Nevada, New Hampshire, New Jersey, Rhode Island, Vermont, West Virginia 3. East Coast 4. Texas: 155, Oklahoma: 62, Kansas: 96, Nebraska: 57, Iowa: 51, South Dakota: 36

Make a Tornado in a Jar

Here is your chance to safely see a tornado up close. Just mix it up and watch as a spinning vortex takes shape!

Directions

 1 Fill the clear jar three-fourths full of water.

Materials

Clear glass or plastic jar with a screw-on lid

Water

1 teaspoon dish soap

1 teaspoon vinegar

Food coloring

 2 Add a teaspoon of dish soap, a teaspoon of vinegar, and one or two drops of food coloring to the jar.

3 Screw on the lid. Tightly grip the top and bottom of the jar. Move it rapidly in a circular motion.

4 Stop moving and watch your tornado touch down.

Explain It!

Using what you learned in the book, can you explain what happened and why? If you need help, turn back to page 11.

True Statistics

Most tornadoes formed in a single outbreak:
349 across 21 states in April 2011

Highest tornado wind speed ever measured:
318 miles per hour (512 kph, Oklahoma 1999)

Average number of people killed by a tornado in the United States each year: 76

Forward speed of the fastest-moving tornado:
73 miles per hour (117 kph) (The Tri-State Tornado of 1925)

Most tornadoes to form in a single month:
817 around the world (April 2011)

Greatest number of tornadoes spawned from a hurricane: 117 tornadoes spawned from Hurricane Ivan in 2004

Did you find the truth?

T More tornadoes are reported in the United States than in any other country.

F Tornadoes are most likely to appear at dawn.

Resources

Other books in this series:

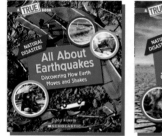

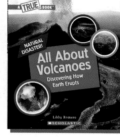
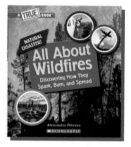

You can also look at:

Carson, Mary Kay. *Inside Tornadoes.* New York: Sterling, 2010.

Gregory, Josh. *If You Were a Kid Surviving a Hurricane.* New York: Children's Press, 2018.

Raum, Elizabeth. *Can You Survive Storm Chasing? An Interactive Survival Adventure.* Mankato, Minnesota: Capstone Press, 2011.

Rice, William B. *Tornadoes.* Huntington Beach, California: Teacher Created Materials, 2009.

Simon, Seymour. *Tornadoes.* New York: HarperCollins, 2001.

Tarshis, Lauren. *I Survived: The Joplin Tornado, 2011.* New York: Scholastic, 2015.

Glossary

atmosphere (AT-muhs-feer) the mixture of gases that surrounds a planet

Doppler radar (DAWP-ler RAY-dahr) a device used in weather forecasting to detect rain and wind

drones (drohns) remote-controlled aircraft

front (fruhnt) the area between two air masses in Earth's atmosphere

meteorologists (mee-tee-uh-RAH-luh-jists) scientists who study the weather

precipitation (pri-sip-i-TAY-shuhn) rain, hail, or snow

pressure (PRESH-ur) a force that pushes against an object

projectiles (pruh-jek-TILES) objects launched or thrown through the air

supercells (SOO-pur-sels) severe thunderstorms with rotating winds that can create tornadoes

tornado (tor-NAY-doh) a violent, rotating column of air that extends from a thunderstorm to the ground

vortex (VOR-tex) a spinning, funnel-shaped cloud

Index

Page numbers in **bold** indicate illustrations.

About the Author

Cody Crane is an award-winning children's writer, specializing in nonfiction. She studied science and environmental reporting at New York University. She always wanted to be a scientist but discovered that writing about science could be just as fun as doing the real thing. She lives in Houston, Texas, with her husband and son.